MIHAI EMINESCU

(1850-1889)

The Greatest Romanian Romantic Poet

By Keelan Thome

Table of content

The Evening Star

Why do you wail, o forest trees

How many a time, beloved

Legendary queen

A dacian's prayer

O mother

Beats the moon upon my window

Separation

Midst the dense old forest stout

What is love?

Calin

Epigones

Sonnet I

Sonnet II

Sonnet III

Sonnet IV

Sonnet V

Sonnet VI

Satire I

Satire II

Satire III

Satire IV

Delilah (Satire V)

'Tis eve on the hillside

You never knew my soul

Of all the ships

Fair love, our mutual friend

Angel and Demon

So long, dear one, since you departed

Return

One wish alone have I

The Evening Star

There was, as in the fairy tales,
As ne'er in the time's raid,
There was, of famous royal blood
A most beautiful maid.

She was her parents' only child,
Bright like the sun at noon,
Like the Virgin midst the saints
And among stars the moon.

From the deep shadow of the vaults
Her step now she directs
Toward a window; at its nook
Bright Evening-star expects.

She looks as in the distant seas
He rises, darts his rays
And leads the blackish, loaded ships
On the wet, moving, ways.

To look at him every night
Her soul her instincts spur;
And as he looks at her for weeks
He falls in love with her.

And as on her elbows she leans
Her temple and her whim
She feels in her heart and soul that
She falls in love with him.

And ev'ry night his stormy flames
More stormily renew
When in the shadow of the castle
She shows to his bright view.

And to her room with her slow steps
He bears his steps and aims

Weaving out of his sparkles cold
A toil of shaking flames.

And when she throws upon her bed
Her tired limbs and reposes,
He glides his light along her hands
And her sweet eyelash closes.

And from the mirror on her shape
A beam has spread and burns,
On her big eyes that beat though closed
And on her face that turns.

Her smiles view him; the mirror shows
Him trembling in the nook
For he is plunging in her dream
So that their souls may hook.

She speaks with him in sleep and sighs
While her heart's swelled veins drum:
-"O sweet Lord of my fairy nights,
Why comes thou not? Come!

Descend to me, mild Evening-star
Thou canst glide on a beam,
Enter my dwelling and my mind
And over my life gleam!"

And he listens and trembles and
Still more for her love craves
And as quick as the lightning he
Plunges into the waves.

The water in that very spot
Moves rolling many rings
And out of the unknown, dark, depth
A superb young man springs.

As on a threshold o'er the sill
His hasty steps he leads,

Holds in his hand a staff with, at
Its top, a crown of reeds!

A young Voivode he seems to be
With soft and golden hair;
A blue shroud binds in a knot on
His naked shoulder fair.

The shade of his face is of wax
And thou canst see throughout -
A handsome dead man with live eyes
That throw their sparkles out.

-"From my sphere hardly I come to
Follow thy call and thee,
The heaven is my father and
My mother is the sea.

So that I could come to thy room
And look at thee from near
With my light reborn from waves my
Fate toward thee I steer.

O come, my treasure wonderful
And thy world leave aside;
For I am Evening-star up from
And thou wouldst be my bride.

In my palace of coral I'll
Take thee for evermore
And the entire world of the sea
Will kneel before thy door."

-"O thou art beautiful as but
In dreams an angel shows,
The way though thou hast oped for me
For me's for ever close.

Thy port and mien and speech are strange
Life thy gleams don't impart,

For I'm alive and thou art dead
And thy eyes chill my heart."

Days have past since: but Evening-star
Comes up again and stays
Just as before, spreading o'er her
His clear, translucent rays.

In sleep she would remember him
And, as before, her whole
Wish for the Master of the waves
Is clinching now her soul.

-"Descend to me, mild Evening-star
Thou canst glide on a beam,
Enter my dwelling and my mind
And over my life gleam!"

He hears: and from the dire despair
Of such an woeful weird
He dies, and the heavens revolve
Where he has disappeared.

Soon in the air flames ruddy spread,
The world in their grip hold;
A superb form the spasms of the
Chaotic valleys mold.

On his locks of black hair he bears
His crown a fierce fire frames;
He floats as he really comes
Swimming in the sun's flames.

His black shroud lets develop out
His arms marbly and hale;
He pensively and sadly brings
His face awfully pale.

But his big wonderful eyes' gleam,
Chimerically deep,

Shows two unsatiated spasms
That but into dark peep.

-"From my sphere hardly I come to
Follow thy voice, thy sight;
The bright sun is my father and
My mother is the night.

O come, my treasure wonderful
And thy world leave aside
For I am Evening-star from up
And thou wouldst be my bride.

O come, and upon thy blond hair
Crowns of stars I shall crowd,
And more that all of them, up there,
Thou wild look fair and proud."

-"O thou art beautiful as but
In dreams a demon shows,
The way though hast oped for me
For me's for ever close.

The depths of my breast ache from the
Desire of thy fierce love
My heavy, big eyes also ache
When into them thine shove".

-"But how wouldst thou that I come down?
Know this - for, do I lie? -:
I am immortal, while thou art
One of those that must die!"

-"I hate big words, nor do I know
How to begin my plea;
And although thy discourse is clear
I don't understand thee.

But if thou wantest my flamed love
And that would not be sham,

Come down on this temporal earth,
Be mortal as I am!"

-"I'd lose my immortality
For but one kiss of thine!
Well, I will show thee how much too
For thy fierce love I pine!

Yes, I shall be reborn from sin,
Receive another creed:
From that endlessness to which I
Am tied, I shall be freed!"

And out he went, he went, went out,
Loving a human fay,
He plucked himself off from the sky,
Went for many a day.

Meanwhile, the house-boy, Catalin,
Sly, and who often jests
When he's filling with wine the cups
Of the banqueting guests;

A page that carries step by step
The trail of the Queen's gown,
A wandering bastard, but bold
Like no one in the town;

His little cheek - a peony
That under the sun stews;
Watchful, just like a thief, he sneaks
In Catalina's views.

-"How beautiful she grew" - thinks he -
"A flower just to pluck!
Now, Catalin, but now it is
Thy chance to try thy luck!"

And by the way, hurriedly, he
Corners that human fay:
-"What's with thee, Catalin? Let me
Alone and go thy way!"

-"No! I want thee to stay away
From thoughts that have no fun.
I want to see thee only laugh,
Give me a kiss, just one!"

-"I don't know what it is about
And, believe me, retire!
But for one Evening-star up from
I've kept my strong desire!"

-"If thou dost not know I could show
Thee all about love's balm!
Only, don't give way to thy ire
And listen and be calm.

So as the hunter throws the net
That many birds would harm,
When I'll stretch my left arm to thee,
Enlace me with thy arm.

Under my eyes keep thine and don't
Let them move on their wheels
And if I lift thee by the waist
Thou must lift on thy heels.

When I bend down my face, to hold
Thine up must be thy strife;
So, to each other we could throw
Sweet, eager, looks for life.

And so that thou have about love
A knowledge true and plain,
When I stoop to kiss thee, thou must
Kiss me too and again."

With much bewilderment her mind
The little boy's word fills,
And shyly and nicely now she
Wills not, and now she wills.

And slowly she tells him:- "Since thy
Childhood I've known thy wit,
And as thou art and glib and small
My temper thou wouldst fit.

But Evening-star sprung from the calm
Of the oblivion,
Though, gives horizon limitless
To the sea lone and dun.

And secretly, I close my eyes
For my eyelash tears dim
When the waves of the sea go on
Travelling toward him.

He shines with love unspeakable
So that my pains he'd leach,
But higher and higher soars, so
That his hand I'd ne'er reach.

Sadly thrusts from the worlds which from
My soul his cold ray bar...
I shall love him for ever and
For ever he'll rove far.

Like the unmeasured steppes my days
Are deaf and wild, therefore,
But my nights spread a holy charm
I understand no more!"

-"Thou art a child! Let's go! Through new
Lands our own fate let's frame!
Soon they shall have lost our trace and
Forgot even our name!

We shall be both wise, glad and whole
As my judgement infers
And thou wouldst not long for thy kin
Nor yearn for Evening-stars!"

Then Evening-star went out. His wings
Grow, into heavens dash,
And on his way millenniums
Flee in less than a flash.

Below, a depth of stars; above,
The heaven stars begem, -
He seems an endless lightning that
Is wandering through them.

And from the Chaos' vales he sees
How in an immense ring
Round him, as in the World's first day,
Lights from their sources spring;

How, springing, they hem him like an
Ocean that swimming nears...
He flees carried by his desire
Until he disappears.

For that region is boundless and
Searching regards avoids
And Time strive vainly there to come
To life from the dark voids.

'Tis nought. 'Tis, though, thirst that sips him
And which he cannot shun,
'Tis depth unknown, comparable
To blind oblivion.

-"From that dark, choking, endlessness
Into which I am furled,
Father, undo me, and for e'er
Be praised in the whole world!

Ask anything for this new fate
For with mine I am through:
O hear my prayer, O my Lord, for
Thou gives life and death too.

Take back my endlessness, the fires
That my being devour
And in return give me a chance
To love but for an hour!

I've come from Chaos; I'd return
To that my former nest...
And as I have been brought to life
From rest, I crave for rest!"

-"Hyperion, that comest from
The depths with the world's swarm,
Do not ask signs and miracles
That have no name nor form.

Thou wantest to count among men,
Take their resemblance vain;
But would now the whole mankind die
Men will be born again.

But they are building on the wind
Ideals void and blind;
When human waves run into graves
New waves spring from behind.

Fate's persecutions, lucky stars,
They only are to own;
Here we know neither time nor space,
Death we have never known.

From the eternal yesterday
Drinks what to-day will drain
And if a sun dies on the sky
A sun quickens again.

Risen as for ever, death though
Follows them like a thorn
For all are born only to die
And die to be reborn.

But thou remainest wheresoe'er
Thou wouldst set down or flee.
Thou art of the prime form and an
Eternal prodigy.

Thou wilt now hear the wondrous voice
At whose bewitched singing
Mounts woody get skipping to skies
Into sea Island sinking!

Perhaps thou wilt more: show in deeds
Thy sense of justice, might,
Out of the earth's lumps make an empire
And settle on its height!

I can give thee millions of vessels
And hosts; thou, bear thy breath
O'er all the lands, o'er all the oceans:
I cannot give thee death.

For whom thou wantest then to die?
Just go and see what's worth
All that is waiting there for thee
On that wandering earth!"

His first dominion on the sky
Hyperion restores
And like in his first day, his light
All o'er again he pours.

For it is evening and the night
Her duty never waives.
Now the moon rises quietly
And shaking from the waves,

And upon the paths of the groves
Her sparkles again drone...
Under the row of linden-trees
Two youths sit all alone.

-"O darling, let my blessed ear feel
How thy heart's pulses beat,
Under the ray of thy eyes clear
And unspeakably sweet.

With the charms of their cold light pierce
My thought's faery glades,
Pour an eternal quietness
On my passion's dark shades.

And there, above, remain to stop
Thy woe's violet stream,
For thou art my first source of love
And also my last dream!"

Hyperion beholds how love
Their eyes equally charms:
Scarcely his arm touches her neck,
She takes him in her arms.

The silvery blooms spread their smells
And their soft cascade strokes
The tops of the heads of both youths
With long and golden locks.

And all bewitched by love, she lifts
Her eyes toward the fires
Of the witnessing Evening-star
And trusts him her desires:

-"Descend to me, mild Evening-star
Thou canst glide on a beam,
Enter my forest and my mind
And o'er my good luck gleam!"

As he did it once, into woods,
On hills, his rays he urges,
Guiding throughout so many wilds
The gleaming, moving, surges.

But he falls not as he did once
From his height into swells:
-"What matters thee, clod of dust, if
'Tis me or someone else?

You live in your sphere's narrowness
And luck rules over you -
But in my steady world I feel
Eternal, cold and true!"

O Remain

O remain, dear one, I love you,
Stay with me in my fair land,
For your dreamings and your longings
Only I can understand.
You, who like a prince reclining
Over the pool with heaven starred;
You who gaze up from the water
With such earnest deep regard.

Stay, for where the lapping wavelets
Shake the tall and tasseled grass,
I will make you hear in secret
How the furtive chamois pass.

Oh, I see you wrapped in magic,
Hear your murmur low and sweet,
As you break the shallow water
With your slender naked feet;

See you thus amidst the ripples
Which the moon's pale beams engage,
And your years seem but an instant,
And each instant seems an age."

Thus spake the woods in soft entreaty;
Arching boughs above me bent,
But I whistled high, and laughing
Out into the open went.

Now though even I roamed that country
How could I its charm recall ...
Where has boyhood gone, I wonder,
With its pool and woods and all?

Why do you wail, o forest trees

Why do you wail o forest trees,
Forest, without rain or breeze,
Your branches ill at ease? "
"How indeed should I not wail
When the hours of Sumner fail !
Nights grow longer, days get short,
On my branches few leaves caught,
And the winds with bitter sword
Drive my choristers abroad;
Autumn winds that forests flay,
Winter near, spring far away.
How indeed should I not groan
When my singing birds have flown,
And across the frozen sky
Flocks of swallows hurry by,
And with them my fancies fly
Leaving me alone to sigh;
Hurly on as time in flight
Turning day half into night,
Time that o'er the forest rings
With a fluttering of wings...
And they pass and leave me cold,
Nude and shivering and old;
For my thoughts with them have flown,
And with them my gladness gone!

How many a time, beloved

How many a time, beloved, no longer do I know,
There seems to spread before me a sea of ice and snow;
And not a single star does in the heaven shine,
Only the yellow quite far away ... a sign.
While o'er the drifted waste of frozen ocean there
A bird with weary wings hangs In the winter air.
Its mate has gone ahead, and left it all alone,
Together with a flock that to the west has flown.
And so it gazes after, with tired, straining eyes,
But is no longer sorry now, nor glad ... and dies,
While do its parting dreams the happy past pursue.

....

Day by day I'm farther, beloved one, from you,
And slowly, cold and darkness to take me for their prey ...
While you fly on for ever, midst time's eternal day.

Legendary queen

Sparkling haze, across the heavens
Rising slow the silver moon,
She has gathered from the water
And upon the pastures strewn.

In the valley many flowers
On the cobwebs jewels strung,
Countless gems, of countless colours,
On the cloak of evening hung.

O'er the lake the clouds in passing,
Cast a soft transparent shade,
Which the ripples rolling boulders
With their radiance invade.

Came at night a little maiden
Silently the reeds among,
And a rose of flaming scarlet
On the water surface flung.

For her own sweet image gazing,
Marvelled how the ripples stirred...
Ay, that lake is long enchanted
By the saint Mercury's word.

Flung a rose of flaming scarlet
That the water's mirror blurred...
Scarlet roses are enchanted
By the saint Veneryts word.

Long she gazes. Hair soft, golden,
O'er her face the moon's pale light,
While within her eyes of violet
All times fairy tales unite.

A dacian's prayer

When death did not exist, nor yet eternity,
Before the seed of life had first set living free,
When yesterday was nothing, and time had not begun,
And one included all things, and all was less than one,
When sun and moon and sky, the stars, the spinning earth
Were still part of the things that had not come to birth
And You quite lonely stood... I ask myself with awe,
Who is this mighty God we bow ourselves before.

Ere yet the Gods existed already He was God
And out of endless water with fire the lightning shed;
He gave the Gods their reason, and joy to earth did bring,
He brought to man forgiveness, and set salvation's spring.
Lift up your hearts in worship, a song of praise en freeing,
He is the death of dying, the primal birth of being.

To him I owe my eyes that I can see the dawn,
To him I owe my heart wherein is pity born;
When ever I hear the tempest, I hear him pass along
Midst multitude of voices raised in a holy song,
And yet of his great mercy I beg still one behest:
That I at last be taken to his eternal rest.

Be curses on the fellow who would my praise acclaim.
But blessings upon him who does my soul defame;
Believe no matter whom who slanders my renown,
Give power to the arm that lifts to strike me down
Let him upon the earth above all others loom
Who steals away the stone that lies upon my tomb.

Hunted by humanity, let me my whole life fly
Until I feel from weeping my very eyes are dry;
Let everyone detest me no matter where I go,
Until from persecution myself I do not know;
Let misery and horror my heart transform to stone,
That I may hate my mother, in whose love I have grown;
Till hating and deceiving for me with love will vie,
And I forget my suffering, and learn at last to die.

Dishonoured let me perish, an outcast among men;
My body less than worthy to block the gutter then,
And may, o God of mercy, a crown of diamonds wear
The one who gives my heart the hungry dogs to tear,
While for the one who in my face does callous fling a cloud
In your eternal kingdom reserve a place, o God.

Thus only, gracious Father, can I requitance give
That you from your great bounty vouched me the joy to live
To gain eternal blessings my head I do not bow,
But rather ask that you in hating compassion show.
Till comes at last the evening, your breath will mine efface,
And into endless nothing I go, and leave no trace.

O mother

O mother, darling mother, lost in time's formless haze
Amidst the leaves sweet rustle you call my name always;
Amidst their fluttering murmur above your sacred grave
I hear you softly whisper when ever the branches wave;
While o'er your tomb the willows their autumn raiment heap...
For ever wave the branches, and you for ever sleep.

When I shall die, beloved, do not beside me mourn,
But break a branch of blossom that does the lime adorn,
And take it very softly, and plant it at my head;
I'll feel its shadow growing as on the soil it's shed,
And watered by the tears that you for sorrow weep...
For ever grow that shadow, and I for ever sleep.

And should it be together that we shall die one day,
They shall not in some cemetery our separate bodies lay,
But let them dig a grave near where the river flows
And in a single coffin them both together close;
That I to time eternal my love beside me keep...
For ever wail the water, and we for ever sleep.

Beats the moon upon my window

Beats the moon upon my window
Down the same untroubled lane.
Only you are never passing,
Nevermore beyond my pane.

And the same prune trees in blossom
Reach their branches o'er the fence,
But the hours the past has taken
Never shall again come thence.

Other is your soul's intention,
Other eyes you have today,
Only I who am unchanging
Tread for ever that same way.

O, how slim and young and graceful,
Secretly with paces slow,
Would you come to me at evening
'Neath the hidden hawthorn's bough.

While my arms were clasped about you
It seemed we from the earth had sped;
And we talked great things together,
Though not a word had either said.

Kisses were our single answer,
Many queries, just one task,
While about the world beyond us
Neither had the time to ask.

Aye, little I knew in youth's enchantment
That it is alike absurd
Or to lean against a shadow,
Or believe a woman's word.

And the air still moves my curtain
As it used in times of yore...
Moonlight down the lane uncertain,
Only you come nevermore.

Separation

To not forget our loving, should I a sign implore?
I'd ask for you, but dearest, you are your own no more.
Nor do I beg a flower from in your golden hair;
Forgetfulness, beloved, is but my single prayer.

Oh, what a sad sensation, when joy that soon did wane,
Not swift with it to vanish, but ever here remain!
Down quite a different valley does that same river fret;
The long and silent sameness of immensurable regret
When through this life to wander it has been writ, it seem,
A dream made out of shadow, a shadow made of dream.
From now in my existence what interest can you hold?
Why should one count the ages that o'er the dead are rolled?
No matter whenI I die, this or some later day,
My wish is out o'the mind of all to I pass away,
And you forget the dream that our two hearts endears.
When you look back, beloved, upon the faded years,
Let in the depths of shadow my memory be gone,
As though we midst our loving each other had not known,
As though those hours of wonder in fact we did not live.
That I so deeply love you dear one can you forgive?
My face turned to the desert you left me all alone
And cold beneath my eyelids my eyes have turned to stone
And when at last death's soil my body does reclaim,
Then who on earth will know me or know from whence I came?

A chant of lamentation within cold walls will chime
To beg for me in weeping the peace of endless time
And I would fain that someone quite near to me then came
To whisper to me softly, beloved one, your name
While then... should they my body into the gutter throw,
Still that would be far better than what I suffer now
Afar off in the distance a flock of crows arise
And darken all the heavens before my sightless eyes;
Beyond the earth's steep margin a hurricane does start,
Flinging to the world my dust and to the wind my heart.

Yet as in spring the blossom do you remain the while,

With gentle eyes and humid, and tender childish smile;
So much a child, yet seeming each day to younger grow,
And of my fate know nothing, as I too nothing know.

Midst the dense old forest stout

Midst the dense old forest stout
All the merry birds fly out,
Quit the hazel thicket there
Out into the sunny air,
Round the pool grown high with sedge
Fiy about the water's edge
Where, by little waves deflected,
On its shining face reflected,
Image of the moon is lying,
And of birds of passage flying,
And of stars and heavens blue,
And of swallows not a few,
And my darling's image too.

What is love?

What is love? A lifetime spent
Of days that pain does fill,
That thousand tears can't content,
But asks for tears still.

With but a little glance coquet
Your soul it knows to tie,
That of it's spell you can't forget
Until the day you die.

Upon your threshold does it stand,
In every nook conspire,
That you may whisper hand in hand
Your tale of heart's aspire.

Till fades the very earth and sky,
Your heart completely broken,
And all the world hangs on a sigh,
A word but partly spoken.

It follows you for weeks and weeks
And in your soul assembles
The memory of blushing cheeks
And eyelash fair that trembles.

It comes to you a sudden ray
As though of starlight's spending,
How many and many a time each day
And every night unending.

For of your life has fate decreed
That pain shall it enfold,
As does the clinging water-weed
About a swimmer hold.

Calin

Autumn come, the dead leaves flying,
A cricket somewhere softy crying,
A sad breeze whispering at your window,
The pane with trembling fingers prying,
While you're awaiting gentle sleep
Alone before your fireplace lying.
What made you start and raise your head.
Was is a foot the stairway trying?
Aye, 'tis your lover come at last,
Around your waist his strong arm plying.
Before your face he holds a mirror,
Wherein your loveliness espying,
You gaze upon its image long
And linger, dreaming, smiling, sighing.

I

Over the hill the moon ascends her fiery crown of crimson deep,
Staining the ancient forest red, and the lonely castle keep,
And staining red the tumbling waves that from a murmuring fountain well,
While down the sweeping valley rolls the solemn music of a bell.
Above the river's rocky course rises the castle grim and tall
While, clinging fast against its face, a knight is scaling high the wall;
Clambering up on hands and knees, and holding tight to crack and edge,
Until the rusty bars he breaks that issue from a window ledge.
Silently he passes through, and soft, on tiptoe, does he creep
Into a secret chamber where the wall is hung with shadow deep
And where the starry sky between the bars and tangled creepers gleams
And timidly and unassured the broken moonlight softly streams;
Where strikes the moon the walls and floor are white as though they had been chalked,

But darkness lies where shadows fall, as black as though with charcoal marked.
Down from the ceiling to the floor has an enchanted spider spun
A wonder web, more light and fair than e'er by human weaver done.
It trembles in the silver light as though its veil would surely tear
Beneath the weight of misty gems that shine upon its filet there.
Beyond the web, in magic sleep, the sovereign's lovely daughter lies,
Drenched in the moon's unearthly light, before the knight's enraptured eyes.
Beneath the sheet her form he sees, her sleeping body young and fair,
For the silken coverings hide it but little from his stare,
And here and there her sleeping gown parted a little leaves to show
The secret lovely nakedness of girlish limbs as white as snow.
Upon her pillow's smooth incline her heavy golden hair is laid,
While on her temples gently throb her pulses in a violet shade:
Drawn as though in one straight line, in noble and bewitching grace
Beneath the curtain of lids, her eyes in slumber seem to beat?
While one smooth rounded shapely arm lies nakedly upon the sheet.
Her full and gently moving breast in maiden ripeness tender shows
And through her lips, a bit apart, her burning breath in silence flows.
Her delicate and lovely mouth moves sweetly in a wistful smile,
While over her and round her head a mound of fragrant petals pile.
But now the knight draws near her bed and stretching out his hand he tears
The spider's sparkling wonder web and spills the precious gems it bears.
Upon her beauty's nakedness he feeds his hungry heart's desire
And scarcely can his breast contain the burning ardour of its fire;

Till clasping her to him at last in one long, clinging sweet caress,
His scarlet mouth is set on hers, and on her lips his hot lips press.
Then taking from her hand a ring, glittering with jewels dear,
Turns, and through the moonlit casement goes our dauntless cavalier.

II

When morning comes, and the wondering maid finds that the web is broken through
And in her mirror sees her lips by thirsty kisses bruised and blue,
Sadly she smiles and softly says, while gazing on her image white;
"O dauntless, dark curled fairy prince, come back again to me tonight".

III

Each one of us has private notions about sweet maidens and their ways,
But no man in his sense will doubt that they Love best themselves to praise.
Just as Narciccus saw his face framed in the water's silver glass
And finding he was fair, at once the lover and the loved one was.
If we could only see the maid when she essays her winning airs,
When all alone with with round eyes she at her mirrored image stares,
See the provoking, pouting lips moving to call herself by name,
And she herself more lovable than all the world does soft acclaim;
He that is wise in maidens' ways would read her secret at a glace,
And know the lovely lass has grown aware of her own elegance.

Idol thou, o thief of wits, great blue eyes and golden hair,
The worship of your maiden heart has chosen too an idol fair !
What does she whisper secretly, what words of love does she bestow
Upon the figure mirrored there, which she regards from top to toe?
"A beauteous dream I had indeed, a fairy prince who came by night.
I almost squeezed the life from him, my arm about him clasped so tight.
And thus it is, with outstretched arms, my gaze my image does caress
When I before my mirror stand alone in all my nakedness,
And like a cloak against my sides my heavy hanging golden hair,
When I regard myself and smile, and fain would kiss my shoulder bare,
Until the blood mounts to my face for very shame of my desires,
O fairy prince why don't you come to quench the flame my being fires,
If in my body I rejoice, if I find pleasure in my eyes,
It is because I see 'tis there the wonders of his passion rise;
The love I love I lavish on myself is only of his love a part.
Mouth, learn wisdom's quick restraint, lest you betray my loving heart
Even to him who steals by night to the couch on which his loved one lies,
Be passionate as a woman is, but as an artful child be wise".

IV

So every night the fairy prince does to her bedside softly creep
And with a sweet enchanted kiss awake her gently from her sleep.
And when he to the window goes to flee before the dawn away,
She will retain him with her eyes and humbly pleading she will say:
"O stay, o go not with the dawn, think of the fiery vows you made,

Do not depart, may black-locked prince, o luckless and ill-fated shade.
You will not find in wandering through all the endless ways of space
A soul to love you as I do, you will not find a fairer face.
Sweet is the shadow of your eyes with depth of sadness unsurpassed,
May no one on your, luckless course the evil eye upon you cast".
Then to her bed he comes again, about her waist her his strong arms steal,
She whispers words of tender love, whispers which her fiery kisses seal.
He murmurs "Whisper on, dear love, and let thy eyes' soft mystery
Speak on in meaningless sweet words, that full of meaning are to me.
Life's golden moment, swift as light, as transient as the rising smoke,
I dream entire when with my hands thy mouth and shapely arm I stroke,
When on my breast you lean your head feeling my heart's enamoured beat
And I in passion press my lips upon your rounded shoulder sweet;
And when our thirsty lips unite, I drink thy breath into my soul,
Our hearts grown heavy in our breasts, that each the other's pain console.
When, lost in ecstasy of love, you hold your burning cheek to mine,
And when your long, soft golden hair about my neck you gently twine,
And when at last you close your eyes and generously your kisses give,
Then am I happiest of men, the height of joy superlative...
And you... but no, I have no words, my tongue is tied and cannot move,
I would, and yet I cannot speak... I cannot tell you how I love".
Thus would they talk and so much say, such happiness was in them springing,

Yet often was their discourse checked, their lips so often sweetly clinging,
Thus clasped in close embrace they lay, drinking of lover's joy their fill.
Till silent grew their lips at last, although their eyes were speaking still
And bashfully she covered up her face, with soft confusion red,
And hid her tearful eyes within her shining hair of golden thread.

V

Now white and waxen is your face that ruddy like an apple shone,
And your smooth and lovely cheeks have shrunken grown and thin and wan.
Now from your eyes your silken tresses wipe many a sad despairing tear
That from your broken heart is sent. Disenchanted you appear,
Standing thus before your window, with no word upon your lips.
Now you raise your long wet lashes, and out of the room your sad soul slips,
Soaring up the limpid heavens where the tireless lark does fly.
You would call for him to take you with him up the shining sky.
The bird flies on quite unawares while you with tearful eyes remain,
Your luckless lips devoid of speech, trembling as though in pain.
O do not quench in useless weeping the light that gleams from your blue eyes;
Do not forget that in their tears the secret of their beauty lies.
Thus, silver drops, from heaven's space, the falling stars descend like rain,
But ere they cross the deep blue vault they are each one re-caught again,
For should they weep their tears away the heavens would be blind and bare.
Fruitless is it that you essay to span the lofty dome of air.
The night of moonshine and of stars, of streams like mirrors shining bright

Cannot be likened anyway unto the tomb's dark endless night.
It does but lend your beauty charm if now and then a tear be shed,
But if you drain the fountains dry, how shall they be replenished?
Let the colour gain your cheeks, as proud and lovely as a rose,
Your youthful cheeks that now are pale as violet shaded mountain snows.
Your eyes give back their violet night that all eternity endears,
But which so swiftly destroyed beneath the track of bitter tears.
Who is there who is mad enough to burn on coals an emerald rare,
That all its lovely lustrous shine be lost and squandered in the air?
You veil your eyes' dark brilliancy to waste your beauty unbeguiled,
And knows the world not what it lacks. O weep no more, you hapless child.

VI

O king, with long and tangled beard, like twisted hanks of cotton wool,
There is no wisdom in your brains: with bran and dust your skull is full.
Are you well pleased to be alone, you sorry joker, weak and old,
Poor are you now in very truth, that once had riches beyond words.
Your daughter you have driven out, to some far corner of the earth,
That in a mean and lonely hut to a young prince she should give birth.
In vain you send your messengers to search for her the whole world round,
For not a single one of them can guess the place she may be found.

VII

Grey are the autumn evenings now; the water of the lake is grey,
A thousand ripples cross its face to hide among the reeds away;
While through the forest gently sighs a wind that takes the withered leaves
And shakes them softly to the ground, a passing wind that sadly heaves
The boughs. Till now the forest branches stripped of all their leaves are bare
And does the lonely moon unchecked her beams of silver squander there.
In melancholy harmonies the brook is murmuring its distress
The wailing breeze snaps off a twig and nature dons her saddest dress.
But who is this that wanders down the steep and winding forest track,
This youth who o'er the valley throws his eagle eyes of fiery black?
O dark-haired prince, seven years have passed since when you climbed the castle wall,
Have you forgot the lovely maid that loved you well and gave you all?
Now in the open field he sees a little, bright, bare footed child
Endeavouring to drive along a quacking brood of ducklings wild.
"Good day to you, my lad", he cries... "Good day brave stranger," says the lad.
"Tell me what's your name young man". "Calin, the name my father had.
Whenever I my mother ask whose boy I am she says the same:
A fairy prince your father is, and Calin also is his name".
And as he listens only he knows how his heart leaps up with joy
To see this child that drives the ducks and recognize him as his boy
Hi enters now the narrow hut where, at a wooden bench's end,
A rush light in an earthen pot its feeble yellow light does serend.

Two large round cakes he finds are set to bake upon the hearth's rude stone;
One shoe is flung beneath a beam and one behind the door is thrown.
An old and dented coffee-mill somewhere in a corner lies,
While near the fire a sleek tomcat purrs and cleans its ears and eye
Beneath the icon of a saint, hanging be smoked upon the wall,
A little candela is hung, as poppy seed its flame is small.
Below the icon on a shelf are thyme and mint arranged in heaps,
From which throughout the darkened hut a hot and peppery fragrance seeps.
Upon the dingy plaster walls and on the stone besmeared with clay
The infant, with a charcoal stick, has drawn, to wile the time away,
Pigs with corkscrew curling tails and little trotters drawn like twigs,
The kind that really most become all self-respecting piggie-wigs.
Across the tiny window frame a bladder stretched in place of glass,
Through which but faint and gloomy rays into the cottage dimly pass.
Upon a bed of simple boards, motionless the princess lies,
Her face towards the window turned, but closed in sleep her lovely eyes.
He sits beside her on the bed, he lays his hand upon her brow,
And sadly he caresses her, he sighs and fondles her, and now,
Bending down his lips to her, quietly her name he calls,
Till, opening her drowsy eyes o'er which a fringe of lashes falls,
Terrified she starts and stares, believing it is all a dream;
Fain would she smile but does not dare, she is afraid yet dares not scream.
He lifts her from her narrow bed and holds his arms around her fast,
His heart so beats within his breast he feels that it must burst at last.

She stares at him and still she stares, but not a single world is said
Then laughs with brimming tearful eyes, before this miracle afraid.
Around her finger long and white she twists a mesh of raven hair,
Then falls upon his ready breast to hide from him her blushes there.
He smoothes away the kerchief that wraps and covers up her head,
And tenderly with burning lips does kiss that crown of golden thread.
She raises her face to his, her eyes, in which sparkling tears spring
And fondly their lips unite, and each does to the other cling.

VIII

If through the copper woods you pass, the silver woods shine far away,
There you will hear a thousand throats proclaim the forest's roundelay.
The grass beside the bubbling spring shines like snow in sunlight fair
And blue flowers drenched in moisture rise and tremble in the perfumed air.
It seems the tall and ancient trees have souls beneath their bar concealed,
Souls that oft amid their boughs by singing voices are revealed,
While down the hidden forest glades, beneath the twilight's silver haze,
One sees the rapid brooklets leap along their shining pebbly ways.
In hurrying, gleaming ripples bright, sighing among the flowers they go
And tumbling down the torrent's track murmur and gurgle as they flow,
Swelling in liquid masses clear over the shallow gravel beds,
A swirling, eddying, dancing stream, on which the moon her silver sheds.

Many small blue butterflies, and many a swarm of golden bees
Busy at visiting the honey flowers pass in among the trees,
And a host of darting, shining flies of different kinds and hues
Make the summer air vibrate with colours that the eyes confuse.
Beside the sleepy trembling lake, its waters softly glimmering,
Stands a long table over which the torches' flames are shimmering.
Emperors and empresses from North and South and West and East
Are come to meet the lovely bride and celebrate that weddings feast,
Paladins with golden hair and dragons dressed in wondrous mail,
Magicians and astrologers, and the clown Pepele happy and pale.
Above them all the aged king sits in his royal high-backed chair,
Upon his head he wears a crown, has trimmed his beard and combed his hair,
Bolt upright on cushions high he sits, his sceptre in his hand
And is, lest flies should trouble him, by willow bearing pages fanned.
Now out of the forest's black retreat advances Calin, by his side,
Her hand within her bridegroom's hand, his radiant and smiling bride.
As they come near one hears the leaves rustle beneath her rich long dress.
She has her cheeks flushing with pleasure and her eyes sparkling with joy.
Sweeping almost to the ground billows her soft and golden hair,
Falling about her shapely arms and over her white shoulders bare.
Gracefully indeed she moves, carries herself with noble mien,
Upon her brow she wears a star and in her hair blue flowers are seen.
The king bids all the guests to seat themselves, the feast is then begun.

For bridesmaid does he name the moon, for groomsman names the sun.
The guests about the table sit according to their rank and years,
The cobza and the violin play softly to delighted ears.
But what strange music sounds beside? Low as a swarm of bees it hums.
The guests in wonder stare, but none can tell from whence it comes.
Till they descry a cobweb vast hung like a bridge across the glade
O'er which a multitude of beasts rush by in murmuring cascade.
Ants in hundreds carrying sacks of flour and little lumps of yeast
In their strong mouths, to bake puddings and cakes for the wedding feast,
Bees with honey from the comb and pure gold dust upon their thighs,
From which the woodworm, goldsmith fine, will make fantastic jewelleries.
Till lastly comes the wedding train, a cricket bears the usher's rod,
While round him leaps a host of fleas, their tiny feet in iron shod.
In a portentous velvet robe straddles a great potbellied drone,
Who in a drowsy nasal drawl mimics the priestly monotone.
Grasshoppers pull a nutshell coach, the cobweb shakes as it goes by
Within it, curling his moustache, reclines the bridegroom butterfly.
And after him there comes a host of butterflies of every sort
In light hearted cavalcade, playful, gallant, full of sport.
Mosquitoes form the orchestra, here are beetles, there are snails.
The bride, a timid violet moth, shelters behind her trailing veils.
Upon the table spread, the nimble usher cricket takes a spring,
Rises upon his hind legs, bows, and clicks his spurs so that they ring;

Then coughs and buttons up his coat and says, ere the amazement ceased,
"Pardon us, Lords And Ladies, if we have by yours our wedding feast."

Epigones

When I recall the golden days Romanian poesy has seen,
I sink as in a tide of dreams with ripples luminous, serene,
While all around me softly flows the long and tender flood of spring.
I see that boundless ocean night o'er which the stars spread out their sails,
Days with three suns upon their brows, and verdant groves with nightingales,
Clear springs that overflow with thought, and songs like rivers bubbling.

I see the poets who have built a language like a honeycomb:
Cichindeal, the golden mounthed, Mumulean, deep sorrow's home,
Prale strange and twisted one and Daniil, the sad and small,
Vacarescu, sweetly singing love songs of the springs that pass,
Cantemir upon the cloth planning out in knives and glass,
And Beldiman bold trumpeting of enemies in battle fall.

Sihleanu, silver lyre, Donici who was reason's nest,
How as rarely comes to happen, meditating, oft is dressed
In ears that are as donkey's long, or horns, or some such other guise;
Where is his so sagacious ox, and where his fox with cunning wiles?
They all have passed along the road that reaches on for endless miles,
With Pann they're gone, Pepelea's child, as clever as a proverb wise.

Eliad built his songs from dreams and out of legends' ancient glow,
From reding much the holy books, far prophecies of bitter woe,
Truth bathed in myth, or like the sphinx imbued with wisdom's sunset gleam,
Mountain strange, with face of stone, that stands amid the gale of time,

And still today before the world an undeciphered riddling rhyme,
Rears up its head of towering rock amidst the clouds' unending stream.

Bolliac sings of slavedom days, and slavery's heavy brazen bands;
And warrior nations flock to arms where dark Cirlova's banner stands,
Before the present's eyes he makes forgotten ages to appear;
Like Byron, who did loud awake the savage wind of passion's pain,
Pale Alexandrescu who put out the sacred lamp of hope again
Deciphering age-long chaos in the ruin of a single year.

Upon a bed with snow-white shroud, aye, swanlike in her death,
Reclined the maid with lashes long, sweet voice, and gentle breath;
Her life was one continual spring, her dying but one soft regret,
And there her poet lover stood, bound in her fresh young beauty's spell
And from his lyre sweet music poured, and from his eyes the hot tears fell;
From such a source Bolintineanu did tenderly his songs beget.

Muresan shakes rusty chains when his voice is rised in ire
And with his hand benumbed and lame can snap a hawsers threefold wire;
He calls the very stones to life, as did the ancient myth narrate,
Sings the mountains and their pain, the pine-trees and their destiny;
For all his poorness mighty rich, shines like a planet fearlessly,
The priest of our awakening, the prophet of the signs of fate.

Negruzzi wipes away the dust from parchment that the past records
Within whose mouldy pages lie the tales of far Roumanian lords

In curious letters traced of old by trembling hand of many a clerk;
Dipping his brush in the secret well of the hues of history's days gone past,
He takes those times' canvasses and touches them to life at last
Portraying perhaps some prince who ruled the land in ages dark.

And now that of all our poets, the ever young, the always happy,
Who doina sings upon the leaves, as from a flute he pours his lay,
Alecsandri the merry heart, who does his sparkling story tell
As though he might be threading pearls upon a star-beam as it goes;
A luminous and glowing stream of gems that through the ages flows,
And laughs maybe amid his tears while singing what Dridri befell.

Or dreaming of a shadow pale, with folded wings of silver white,
And eyes that like legends with glow a deep and mystic light,
A smile as pure as Mary's own, and a voice like the sound of bells,
He places on her starry brow a diadem with jewels sown;
To rule a rebel world of men, he sets her on a golden throne,
And from his overflowing love the poet's vision softly wells.

Or dreaming when the shepherd lad soft pipes sweet doina's plaintive strain,
A dream of waters deep, of cliffs that rise sublime above the plain,
A dream of ancient forests dark which rest upon the mountainst brow,
He wakes again within our hearts the yearning for our father's land
Till history like an icon fair takes form beneath his skillful hand
And mighty Stephen, sombre lord, comes back again to live an'now.

....
.

And here are we, the epigones, of fickle feeling, broken lyre,
Devoid of days, but passions strong, with aged hearts and ugly, dire
And mocking mask, with which to hide a face both hard and lined with hate.
Our God naught but a shadow show, our country's name an idle sound,
Who seek to hide our emptiness in works of varnish without ground,
You trusted in your art, but we believe in neither self nor fate.

And therefore sacred are your words and destined to eternity,
For in your minds were they conceived and by your flooded hearts set free;
Great souls have you, and ever fresh you keep your youth though you grow old
The world has turned its wheel about, the future lies within your hand,
We are the past; like shapeless trees forlorn and desolate we stand;
And all our works are false and faint, and meaningless and cold.

Lost in your dreams you stood apart, conversing with ideals high;
We smear the sea with painted waves, we patch with tinsel stars the sky;
And this because our heaven is grey, the sea is frozen round our shores.
You follow with tumultuous flight the mounted glory of your thought
And in among the gleaming stars on sky-born wings you lightly sport,
While up the comets' blazing track your spirit in its swiftness soars

Pale wisdom, understanding's child, her sacred taper burning gold,
Her royal smile as of a star that never sets, that grows not old,
Unshades her light to guide your path, to make secure your flowery road.
Your soul is of the angels born, your heart a silver lute becomes,
Across whose strings a song is stirred, the mellow wind of poetry strums;
And to your eyes the earth is built, an icon hanging kings' abode.

But we to whom no vision comes look out with barren sightless stare
We ape the feelings we have not, we see false pictures everywhere;
We call you poets mystic fools and fitting subjects for our mirth.
All is convention: truth today, tomorrow will become a lie.
Aye, you have fought your fight in vain, the present does the past deny;
You, who have dreamt of golden days upon this grey, this bitter earth.

Life has no other scope than death, and after death is life again,
No other reason has the world, no gap within the endless chain;
Men raise up worshipped immages, build systems that they deem exact,
And call them beautiful or good, according to their varying lights,
Dividing into many kinds their fine philosophies and rites
And casting fancy's finery upon the naked flesh of fact.

Tell me what is holy thought? A luminous but misty look
Of formless nonexistings set in a sad and tangled book
Made to confuse the minds of men, if they should chance to read therein.
And what is poetry? An angel pale with crystal gaze,
Voluptuous pictures, trembling sounds. With heavenly toys the poet plays --
A robe of purple and of gold laid on a mortal creature's skin.

I bid farewell to all you poets dreaming fanciful fantastic dreams,
Who gave the rolling waves their music and the stars their silver beams,
Who built upon this world of clay a greater world where thought is free;
Today our heads are laid in dust, behold, tomorrow death is here
Genius, dullard, sound and soul, the common end of all is near,
The earth is naught but flying dust... and of this flying dust are we.

Sonnet I

Loving in secret, I did silence hold
Deeming in this your clemency would dwell,
For when my searching eyes on yours fell
A world of shattered dreams they did behold.

I can no more. My aching love must tell
The mystery that does my heart enfold,
I wish I could drown within the radiance cold
Of that sweet soul that knows my own so well.

But look, my lips are parched with despair,
A thirsty fever does my eyes infest,
Sweet maiden, you, with long and golden hair.

But let your gentle breath my anguish wrest,
Your smile, with drunken joy, my soul ensnare;
Oh, end my pain at last... come to my breast.

Sonnet II

Without 'tis autumn, the wind beats on the pane
With heavy drops, the leaves high upwards sweep.
You take old letters from a crumpled heap,
And in one hour have lived your life again.

Musing, in this sweet wise the moments creep;
You pray no caller will your door attain;
Better it is when dreary falls the rain
To dream before the fire I awaiting sleep.

And thus alone, reclining in my chair,
The fairy Dochia's tale comes to my mind
While round me haze is gathering in the air.

Then softly down the passage footsteps wind,
Faint, sound of rustling silk upon the stair...
And now my eyes cold, tapering fingers bind.

Sonnet III

The years have sped, and time still swiftly flies
Since that first sacred hour in which we met;
But how we loved I can no more forget,
Sweet wonder with cold hands and such big eyes.

O, come again ! Your words inspire me yet,
While your soft gaze upon me gently lies,
That neath its ray new life in me shall rise,
And you new songs upon my lyre beget.

When you come near to me you little know
How soothed my heart is then, as though with balm,
As when some star does in the heavens show;

Your childish smile so full of tender charm
Has power to quench this life drawn out in woe
And fill my eyes with fire, my soul with calm.

Sonnet IV

When even the inner voice of thought is still,
And does some sacred chant my soul endear,
'Tis then I call to thee; but will you hear?
Will from the floating mists your form distil?

Will night its tender power of wonder rear
And your great, peaceful eyes their light fulfil,
That of the rays that bygone hours spill
To me as in a dream you do appear?

But come to me... come near, come still more near...
Smiling you bend to gaze into my face
While does your sigh gentle love make clear.

Upon my eyes I feel your lashes' trace,
O love, for ever lost, for ever dear,
To know the aching thrill of your embrace!

Sonnet V

The years have passed like clouds across the dale;
The years have gone and will return no more,
For they no longer move me, as the lore
Of legend, and of song, and doina's tale
Brought wonder to my boyish brow of yore,
And mystery its meaning half unveil.
Your shade falls round me now to no avail,
O secret twilight hour on evening's shore.

To tear a sound out of the life that's gone,
To stir within my soul again its thrill
My hand upon the silent lyre is numb.

Ay, all is lost beneath youth's horizon,
The tender voice of bygone days is still,
While time rolls out behind me... night has come.

Sonnet VI

Mighty Venice now has fallen low,
One hears no songs, no sound of festive balls;
On steps of marble and through gateways falls
The pallid moon's unearthly silver glow.

Okeanos there his sorrow calls...
In him alone eternal youth does blow,
Yet on his bride would he his breath bestow,
The waves break plaintively against the walls.

The town is silent as a burial ground;
Only the priests of bygone days remain,
Saint Mark tolls sinister the midnight round;

In sombre tones his slow sibylline strain
He nightly speaks with smooth and cadenced sound;
"The dead, my child, no more come back again".

Satire I

When my eyes are weighed with sleep I quench the evening candle's glow
And leave the ticking clock alone the path of time to go
When from my square of window-pane I draw the curtain to one side
The climbing moon pours in and floods the room with her voluptuous light;
Then from the night of memory in answer to her summons steal
An endless host of sorrows pale that we have lived but now scarce feel.

Moon, fair ruler of the sea, over the sky's round vault you glide,
The sight of you recalls the grief's that locked within man's bosom bide;
Beneath thy virgin glow are there a thousand deserts glittering,
And thousand forest shades conceal the wells from which their waters spring!
Over how many million waves extends thy timeless empery
When on your way you sail above the lonely wonder of the sea!
How many flowers besprinkled fields, how many a walled and peopled place
Have known your proud despotic charm when they but looked upon your face!
Into how many thousand rooms you peered as now in mine you peer,
How many thousands brows has lit the flooded glory of thy sphere!
I see a king sit down to plot earth's destiny for endless days
While here the trembling beggar-man plans for the morrow scarcely lays...

Different the lots these twain have drawn out the secret urn of fate
Alike they fall beneath thy sway, alike inherit death's estate;
What're they be they come alike under human passions' rule,
So as the weak man is the strong, so as the genius is the fool.
One searches on the mirror's face a novel way to curl his hair,

Another roves through time and space to track truth to her hidden lair,
Pilling endless loads of lore from ancient learning's yellow page
And nothing down the thoughts and names that sped across some bygone age.
Another from his counting house controls a nation's destinies
And figures gold his ships have brought across a score of troubled seas.
And here the old philosopher, his coatis torn, and does a web of logic spin.
Shivering with cold he buttons up his torn and ragged gown,
Turns up the collar round his neck, presses his cotton ear-plugs down;
Dried up and twisted as he is, of no importance does he stand
And yet he holds the universe within the ambit of his hand;
Within the confine of his brain the future and the past unite
And with his science he lays bare the secrets of eternal night.
As Atlas was of old declared to bear the sky upon his back,
So does our philosopher the world within a cipher tack.
The moon looks in and sheds its beams a pile of ancient books upon,
He sets his mind to roving back across a thousand ages gone
Into the time are things began, when being and not being still
Did not exist to plague man's mind, and there was neither life nor will,
When there was nothing that was hid, yet all things darkly hidden were,
When self-contained was uncontained and all was slumber everywhere.
Was there a heavenly abyss? Or yet unfathomable sea?
There was no mind to contemplate an uncreated mystery.
Then was the darkness all so black as seas that roll deep in the earth,
As black as blinded mortal eye, and no man yet had come to birth,
The shadow of the still unmade did not its silver threads unfold,
And over an unending peace unbroken empty silence rolled!...
Then something small in chaos stirred... the very first and primal cause.

And God the Father married space and placed upon confusion laws.
That moving something, small and light, less than a bubble of sea spray,
Established through the universe eternal and unquestionable sway...
And from that hour the timeless mists draw back their dark and hanging folds.
And law in earth and sun and moon essential form and order moulds.
After that day in endless swarms countless flying worlds have come
Out of the soundless depth of space, each drawn towards its unknown home,
Have come in shining colonies rising from out infinity,
Attracted to the universe by strange and restless urge to be,
while we, inheritors of space, the children of this world of awe,
Are raising witless heaps of sand upon our little earthy floor;
Microscopic nations rise with warrior and king and seer,
Throughout the years our fortunes wax, until we have forgotten fear.
We, flies, that for a single day buzz in a measured world and small,
Suspended in the midst of time, careless and forgetting all
That this frail world in which we trust is only flung momentarily between the darkness that is past and all the darkness yet to be.
Just as the motes of dust enjoy their kingdom in the lamplight's ray,
Thousands specks that are no more when once that beam has passed away
So, in the midst of endless night, we have our little time to spend,
Our moment snatched from chaos, which did not yet come to an end.
But when our beam at last goes out, our world will suddenly disperse
Amidst the dark that ever hangs around this whirling universe.

Yet not within the present day stays the philosopher's quick thought;
One cast of that far-ranging brain a hundred eons of time has caught.
He sees grow small and red and cold the sun that now burns high and proud,
And at last he sees it die closing like a wound stabbed in a cloud.
He sees the rebel planets freeze and headlong plunge about in space
Freed from the ordering of the sun who deep in night has veiled his face.
While o'er earth's altar like a veil eternity its darkness weaves
And one by one pale, faded stars are failing like the autumn leaves.
The body of the universe is stiffened to eternal death
And through the emptiness of space is neither movement, life nor breath.
All falls into not being's night and an unbroken silence reigns
As once again the universe its primal peace and void regains...
....

Commencing with the multitude that swarms uncounted on the ground
And rising to the palace where the Emperor sits with glory crowned,
All are as one, and each is by riddle of his life pursued,
And none can say which man of them is most with misery endued,
For unto all comes each man's lot, to all the fate of each applies.
Little it aids if one of them above his class succeeds to rise
While all the others stay below and gaze on him humble hearts,
For he and they are all unknown, playing the same ephemeral parts.
What reckons fate of their desires, what they would have, or do, or be?
Fate rides as blindly o'er their lives as does the wind across the sea.

Now writers out of every land and all the world high plaudits raise...
What cares the old philosopher? And what to him is all men's praise?
Immortality, people will say! True, all his hard lived days were spent
In clinging to a single thought, as ivy round a tree is bent.
After I die, he tells himself, my name will live to endless time,
From age to age, from mouth to mouth, and carried to the farthest clime,
Unto the farthest realms of earth, and to the world's remotest mind'
Behind the rampart of my works may not my name a refuge find?'
Poor soul ! Do you yourself retain everything that passed your head?
All the dreams that you have dreamed, all the words that you have said?
Little enough: but here there some of images, some bit
Of tattered thought, some phrase, some scrap of yellow paper closely writ.
If you forget the life you had, the things that you have done and seen,
With other men spend fruitless days discovering how it must have been?
Perhaps somewhere in days to come, some green-eyed pedant's gaze will fall
Upon a pile of faded books, himself more faded than them all,
To scan the wonder of your words and weigh them in his niggard scale,
While from their bindings dust will rise and on his glasses spread a veil.
Then will he place your works in rows upon his shelves and summaries
Upon a ragged paper slip; he'll write of your philosophies.

Though you create or sink a world, one end there is to all your toil,
For over you and all your works a spade will heap a mound of soil.

An emperor's head, or one in which a world of wisdom has been stored
Finds ample room within a box composed of four short bits of board....
And all will hasten to attend the honoured funeral you will get,
Splendid in their irony, with posturing of feigned regret ...
And from some carven pulpit tall a nobody will glibly prate;
Not for your honour will he speak, but on his own great gifts dilate
Under the shadow of your name: a windy, pompous, empty speech.

Posterity? What is it but a phantom far beyond your reach!
For who should dream posterity will ever think to talk of you,
Except perhaps in some small tone written with grudging words and few,
Compiled by some old soulless scribe to prove that you were common clay,
A man like any one of them. For fully satisfied are they
To prove you even as themselves. Their learned nostrils wide extending
Dilated with a splendid pride, when at some learned meeting's ending
Your name pedantically is used, knowing beforehand there will be,
Uttered by ironic mouth, some gilded word in praise of thee.
Fallen among these wolfish fools your glory will be torn to shreds,
While all that is not understood will be decried by wagging heads.
Then they will probe your private life, dissecting that, discounting this,
And searching out with eager eyes each little thing you've done amiss,
To make you even as themselves. They will not care for all the light
Your labour poured upon the world, but for the sins and every slight
And human failing they can find, and every petty thing that must
Befall the life of hapless days, of every mortal child of dust.

And every little misery that harassed a tormented mind
Will seem more notable to them than all the truths that you did find.

....

Within a garden's closing walls, where fruit-tree blossom strews the ground,
And over which the full moon sails with all her shining splendour crowned,
Out of the depth of memory's night countless hidden longings rise;
Pain is benumbed as in sleep, we see the world with dreamer's eyes,
For in the calm light of the moon fancy's gates are open wide
And all around us phantoms creep after the candle light has died....
Beneath thy virgin glow, o moon, are thousand deserts glittering
And thousand forest shades conceal the wells from which their waters spring!
Over how many million waves extends thy timeless empery
When on your way you sail above the lonely wonder of the sea!
All who sojourn on this earth, within the iron realm of fate,
Alike are subject to thy sway, alike inherit death's estate!

Satire II

Why does my rhyme-creating pen stand rusting in the ink you ask?
And why has poetry lost its power to tempt me from the daily task?
Why do I sleep my days away, with crushed in yellow pages there
Climbing iambus, trochees swift, and dactyl with the sprightly air?
If you but knew the worries all which fill my waking hours with care,
You'd see I have a wealth of words, enough to choke me and to spare.
But why, I ask, should I begin to shape again the song that's sung
And mould into a form that's new the metal of this wise old tongue?
To twist the secret ecstasies that lie asleep within my breast
To carefully painted couplets which are goods for sale among the rest?
When hungrily I seek the form that best becomes their inward grace,
Why write to suit the world at large a legend on the water's face?

But you will say it would be well that all the corners of the earth
Should come to hear my lovely rhymes, and my name advertise its worth
By tickling the illustrious ears of mighty men of high estate,
Or sweetly flattering verse, perhaps, to lovely ladies dedicate,
And so console my soul's disgust through the prostration of my mind.
Dear friend, the path you indicate is one by many trod I find.
The world can boast today a wealth of that most curious sort of bard
Who his poetry uses as a means to cultivate the great's regard;
By writing dexterous poems which the prowess of his patrons boom,

His songs in coffee-shops are heard, and in my lady's drawing-room.

Knowing the ways of life and how, its narrow road the heart can vex,
Such poets launch their labours 'neath the shelter of the weaker sex,
And dedicate their little books to those whose husbands may by chance
As an appropriate reward their way in politics advance.
Why is it that I do not strive for glory's crown and honours grand?
What fame is there in standing up and preaching to the desert sand?
Today when to his sensual self each mortal man is bounden slave,
Renown is but the idle flag which many thousand dunces wave,
Who, raising up their Idol Gods, a dwarf like to a giant dress,
As bubbles floating in the air amidst an age of nothingness.

Or shall my lyre resound in praise of love? That chain held evenly
Between the hands of lovers two, sometimes the chain that bind three.
What! Suttter on a silver chord where swelling harmony unfolds
And join the operetta where 'tis Menelaus the baton holds?
Women today, like all the world, are often but a kind of school,
Where we can study what is pain, and fraud and make-believe hold rule;
To learn in these academies the votaries of Venus go,
Fond pupils who, the more they learn, the younger and more blatant grow,
Till at the finish of the course we see them in the infant class,
And finally the precious school does into nameless ruin pass.

O, do you still recall the years through which we sweetly dreaming lay
And heard our learned teacher's mumble tailoring time's coat away?
The corpses of the moments gone he reassembled in the past

And searched around for wisdom in the odds and ends that time has cast.
With bland and sleepy murmurings, an endless spring of horum-harum,
Babbling, blinking, pointing out nervum rerum generandum;
The mind's still windlass turning round in heavy, holy pondering,
And now some planet came to view, and now some great Egyptian king.

Me seems I see th'astronomer, yawning away in vaporous rest,
Take out the world from primal night as though wide chaos were a chest,
And spread all time out like a rug; me seems I hear him thoughtfully teach
How eons counted off like beads are threaded on a cotton each,
Talking, talking till the world a whirling in our heads we found
And we like Galileo cried "Upon; my soul, it all goes round."
Till dazed by languages forgotten, planets, dates, scholastic rot.
We mixed our master with a king in who's beard the moths had got,
And gazing at the cobwebs thick that hung from roof and pillar too
We listened to king Ramses, and we dreamed . . . we dreamed sweet eyes of blue.
While in the margin of our books we scribbled verses debonair,
It may be to a rose in bloom or to Clotilda wild and fair;
While round us floated images caught up and tangled in time's net
Now of the sun, now of a king, and now of some domestic pet.
The scratching of our pens gave charm or this array of bending backs
That like the sleepy ocean swelled, or rippled like a field of flax.
And soon obvlion covered all as bent arms pillowed heavy head
Until the clanging class-room bell proclaimed that Ramses must be dead.

Then, the realm of our fancy turned into reality,
While the actual world seemed a mere impossibility.
Now we can see that for a heart loving truth and honesty
The only means becoming are so hard and wiry;
Dreaming is a real danger in this world of commonplace
'Cause if waft by lofty hopes you'll be mocked and put to shame.

And so, my friend, why my good pen rusts in the ink you must not ask
Nor why verse has lost its power to tempt me from the daily task,
Nor why I sleep my days away, with crushed in yellow pages there
Climbing iambus, trochees swift, and dactyl with the sprightly air.
If I should further write, I fear my good contemporaries might laud,
Perhaps my name in verse, and with their praise my work reward;
And if to now I have endured their hatred with a smiling face,
Such prise would seem to me indeed a truly measureless disgrace.

Satire III

A Sultan among those who over a language reign,
Who where the flocks are pastured, there stretches their domain,
Was sleeping on the hillside, his head laid on his arm,
When came to him a vision that did his spirit charm:
He saw the moon that nightly across the heavens ranged
Turn from her wonted journey and to a maiden changed,
He saw her glide towards him, with lovely downcast head,
And there was sorrow in her eyes; but spring bloomed at her tread;
While all the forest trembled, so wondrous was her grace,
And a thrill of silver ripples ran o'er the water's face.
A mist like sparkling diamonds that did the vision daze
Lay on the earth enchanted, a bright illumined haze,
While the sound of whispered music sang through that wonderland,
And o'er the starry heavens a midnight rainbow spanned...
Her hair in raven tresses about her shoulders fell,
And taking his hand in hers, she these grave words did tell:
"Let be our lives united, my pain let yours enfold
That through your sorrow's sweetness my sorrow be consoled...
Writ was it through the ages and all the stars record
That I shall be your mistress, and you shall be my lord."
Now, as the Sultan marvelled, softly she withdrew
And he felt as if within him a wondrous tree up grew;
A that in an instant raised loftily its head
And to the far horizons its thrusting branches spread;
A tree of such a stature that even at midday
The farthest lands and oceans under its shadow lay.
While at the earth's four corners rose up against the sky
Atlas, Caucasus, Taurus and the Balkan mountains high,
The wide Euphrates, Tigris, the Nile, the Danube old,
All 'neath its boughs protecting their mighty waters rolled.
Asia, Europe, Africa and the desert stretching far,
The boats that on the lakes and seas and on the rivers are,
Billowing, boundless corn fields that tossed emerald locks,
And shores, and ships, and harbours with castles on the rocks,

All these spread like a carpet his vision did embrace,
Country next to country set, and race to race...
All these as in a mist of silver did he see,
A vast extending kingdom' neath the shadow of a tree.

The eagle that aspires the sky does dawdle not
With lazy wings, nor in among the branches squat;
And now a wind of conquest the ancient forest fills
And shouts of Allah ! Allah ! echo among the hills,
As though a rising tempest does o'er the ocean roar
The deafening clash of battle, the thunderous clang of war;
Till loudly does the forest to that great gale resound.
And bow before new Rome its branches to the ground.

The Sultan then awakened to find the moon again
Her wonted place had taken above Eskishehr plain,
And sadly to the dwelling of Sheik Edebali turned
And through the window bars a girlish form discerned,
More lightsome than a hazel, a maid who gravely smiled,
Sweet Malcatun the beautiful, Sheik Edebali's child.
And then it was he understood his dream sent by the prophet,
As though a moment he had gained the presence of Mahomet;
He knew that born of this his love would there an empire grow
Of which the tides and boundaries only the sky would know.

Now, as the eagle rises the Sultan's dream came true,
And year by year invincible that gathering kingdom grew,
And year by year the emerald flame flew higher in the blast
As generations came and went and as each sultan passed;
Nor was there any nation could its course forbid
Until up to the Danube rode conquering Bayazid...

From one bank to the other a bridge of boats was cast
And all that host marched over midst fanfare trumpet blast,
The bodyguard of Allah did over the Danube ride
Darkening with their numbers the Rovine countryside,
Swarming tens of thousands spreading their tents immense;
But on the far horizon stood oaks in forest dense.

Now came a company of men, in front a white flag borne,

And Bayazid regarding them enquired with haughty scorn:
"What do you want?"
"We want but peace, and if it be allowed
Our Sire would like to speak awhile with you, great Sultan proud."

At a sign the way was cleared and came towards the tent
A man of calm and simple mien, and with the years bent.
'Isn't Mircea?"
"Yes your Highness !"
"Take heed, for caution warns,
Lest you your crown exchange against a wreath of thorns."
"That you have come, great emperor, no heed what be your aim,
While still at peace I hail you, our greetings that you came;
But, as to your good council, o may the Lord forgive,
If you do dream to win this land by force imperative;
Had you not better return home with calm and peaceful mind
And show in your imperial strength that you are just and kind...
Be the one or be the other, but little does it awe,
Gladly shall we take our fare, either peace or war."
"What, when nations open their gates before my trump
You think my hosts will stumble against a rotten stump?
You do not guess, old dotard, the force my foes deployed.
The West's most noble flower these soldiers have destroyed.
O'er all the cross does shelter, emperors and kings,
The crescent moon ascending its silver shadow flings.
Aye, clad in gleaming armour the cavaliers of Malta,
The Pope who wears three crowns and guards the Holy Altar
Lightning against lightning set and thunder against thunder,
A. storm that fraught the sea with fear and filled the earth with wonder
I needed but to make a sign, a movement of my head
And all the nations in my path in wild disorder fled;
For strong to overthrow the cross did march a mighty host
O'er sea its rule from land to land, on land from coast to coast;
Shattering the peace of earth as it did march along,
Darkening the countryside in tens of thousand strong.
Our lances stood uncounted like a field of growing corn,
And tremble did the ocean o'er which our ships were borne.

At Nicopolis you no doubt saw how many camps were brought,
As though a shining metal wall of swords and spears wrought.
But when I saw their number like the leaves and like the grass,
I swore that I would crush them down and through their mist would pass;
I swore that I would scatter them as wind up flings the foam,
And give my charger hay and oast in the Vatican at Rome ...
Yet you before my legions imagine you can stand,
You ridiculous old dotard, with a bare staff in your hand?"
"To that old dotard, Emperor, aught one courtesy accord
For over all Wallachia 'tis he the chosen lord.
And wiser you would guard your words, nor yet too loudly boast,
Lest should the furious Danube flood engulf your fleeing host.
Along the rolling ages many there were who came
Since Darius Hystaspis of tall immortal fame;
Many there were who flung their dream across the Danube's tide
And set their bridges ship to ship and over them did ride;
Emperors unnumbered, for their cruelty renowned,
Who came to us with hungry eyes for water and for ground;
And though I would not care to brag, tell you this thing I must:
Little time went by ere they were water and were dust.
You boast that on your conquering road no gates for long were closed
Though all the flower the of West your vanguard's march opposed.
But what the high aspiring cause that did their hearts endure?
The vanity of every brave, of every cavalier;
The pomp of noisy conquest; for they had set their vow
To tear the pride from out your heart, the laurels from your brow.
But I defend the poverty and the needs of a struggling land
And therefore all the rocks and streams and hills that guardian stand
And all that grows and moves and breathes to me is ally true,
While every blade of grass and stone is enemy to you,
We have small hosts, yet love of soil had ever power to rid
This flowering land of all its foes. Prepare then Bayazid !"

No sooner had he gone than mighty the commotion !
The forest rang with arms, and rumbled like the ocean,
Amidst the greenwood thousand heads with long and plaited hair,
And several thousands more besides that did bright helmets wear.
While wave on wave of cavalry over the plain did flood
Astride high prancing chargers, their stirrups carved of wood.
Thundering over the battered earth an avalanche they went,
Lances levelled to the charge and bows near double bent;
Till like a shower of shivering light that whistled through the air,
A storm of arrows leapt and sang and flew from everywhere,
A din of blows on armour dealt like rattling of hail,
The noise of hoof and sword and lance, the roar of battle gale.
Unheeded was the Emperor's fury, lion-like his rage,
For hotter still about his troops the fight did deadly wage;
Unheeded did the green flame flutter o'er his stricken ranks
For mightily assailed in front, attacked on both their flanks,
The East's entire battle host was scattered in the fray
And line on line of infantry mown down like summer hay.
A steady rain of arrows fell and sword blows did resound,
While riders dropped on every hand and dead bestrewed the ground.
Till, onset from all sides at once, helpless to fight or fly,
It seemed the very earth was doomed and fallen was the sky...
Mircea himself led on his men midst storm of battle lust
That came, and came, and came, that trod all in the dust;
Their cavalry undaunted, a wall of lances proud
Which through that pagan army streets of daylight ploughed
And laid to earth their thousands like sheaves of ripened corn,
High in the van of conquest Wallachia's banner borne;
As deluge flung from heaven that burst upon the seas,
Till in an hour the heathen were chaff before the breeze
And from that hail of iron fast towards the Danube fled,
While gloriously behind them the Romanian army spread.

Now, while the troops are camping, the sun goes slowly down
Decking the lofty summits with victory's gold crown;
The lightning that from terror had flown out of the sky
Now flashes forth its splendour along the mountains high,

While gradually the planets do up the heaven rear
And o'er the mist-drenched forest the pallid moon appear,
The queen of night and ocean that squanders calm and sleep.
Yet of the sons of Mircea does one still vigil keep,
And on his knee, in musing, beneath the evening star,
He writes to his beloved of Arges village far:
"From deep within Rovine vale,
O lady fair, we bid you hail,
Alas, by letter not by speech,
By sundering distance out of reach.
Yet am I fain to beg of thee
To send by messenger to me
What in your valley fairest be:
The forest with its silver glade,
Thy eyes that long, curled lashes shade.
And I in turn will send to you
The proudest thing that here we view:
This mighty host with banner spread,
The forest, branching overhead,
My helmet with its feathery crest,
My eyes that 'neath their lashes rest.
I have both health and resting place,
Thanks be to Christ and to God's grace,
And now, dear love, I thee embrace".

....

By such an age as this were chroniclers inspired;
But our good age of mountebanks what poet's heart has fired...
In annals of past ages heroes are often found,
But poet, with your late or lyre of dreaming sound
Have you a single patriot to sing about today?
Apollo at the sight of these had hid himself away!
O modern heroes squatting beneath far glory's wing,
Since you are all the fashion I would your prowess sing;
While draped in perfect nullity your praise is writ by those
Who knead the golden ages within the mud of prose.
Musats and Basarabs rest in your sacred shade,
Givers of law and justice, men who our nation made,

Who with the mace and ploughshare spread out our boundaries wide
From seashore to the mountains, and to the Danube side.
The present is not noble? Calling for heroes we?
Is not our street quite famous for dealers in jewellery?
Have not in far Sybaris our manners gained first prize?
From tavern door and alley does glory not arise?
And have we then no heroes, who wield rhetoric slings
Amidst the noisy plaudit of hordes of gutterings?
These pickpockets of honour who on a tightrope dance,
And wear their fancy costumes with perfect elegance.
Of Virtue and The Nation our liberal prates, till sure
His daily life you'd fancy must be as crystal pure?
You'd never dream him being a cafe haunting knave,
Who mocks at his own sermon, so solemn, and so grave.
O could you see the brigand that no conscience has nor soul
With his hang-dog expression and heavy, sullen jaw,
A hunchback, evil-visaged, a spring of cunning greed,
Who spouts out for his comrades some poisoned, nonsense creed.
Upon each lip is Virtue, and in each heart deceit;
A set of wicked monsters and wrong from head to feet
Who round their patrons stagnum, as standing; as those who Gods admire,
Will roll protruding frog eyes, bright with their hearts' aspire.
Such men become our leaders, its laws' our country give,
Men who at best from kindness should in a madhouse live
Clothed each in madmen's jackets, a fool's cap on each head.
But no... they teach us wisdom and make our laws instead.
Patriotism ! Justice !... Such guardians of our State
Despise the laws as nonsense that they themselves create.
As sly as artful foxes will they the benches throng
Frenetically applauding our country game and song;
Then meeting in the Senate each others praises speak
This heavy-throated Bulgar, that long and hook-nosed Greek.
Each claims to be Romanian, whatever mask he wears,
These Bulgo-Greeks pretending that they are Trajan's heirs;
This poison froth, this dung-heap, this foul and filthy brood
Have they indeed inherited our nation's master hood !
The scourings of everywhere, the abortive and the maimed,

All that man rejected and nature has disclaimed,
These crafty, greedy gluttons, these grasping Phanariots
To us they all have flooded and pose as patriots.
Until at last these nothings, this foul and loath full scum,
These cripple-minded stammerers lords of our land become.

Are you then Rome's descendants, you eunuchs and no men?
If you were men in earnest, pity it were that then
This hungry plague of locusts, these creatures crazed and lame
Dare part their lips in public and flatter without shame
Our nations majesty, and make it odious stand,
Dare even speak thy name... o miserable land!
In Paris pleasure houses, there has your congress been;
With jaded, worthless women, in revelry obscene,
In sloth and vulgar rioting you wasted wealth and youth;
In you what could develop, that empty are in sooth?

And, coming back, for wisdom a perfume flask you brought,
A monocle you flourished, a cane for sword you bought.
Withered up before your time, yet childish in your brain,
For scientific knowledge a Bal-Mabil refrain,
And all your father's riches spent on some harlot's shoe:
O admirable and worthy offspring of Romans, you !
And now just look with horror on faces sceptic cold,
What wonder that your falsehoods no more persuasion hold?
When those who speak fine phrases and lofty sermons give
Would simply fill their pockets, that they may lazy live,
Today the polished discourse does little credence know,
But others are the reasons, dear Sirs, is that not so?
Too much have you made riches and power your single aim,
Too much have brought our nation to ridicule and shame,
Too much you mocked the language and customs of this race,
That now at last your mocking does but yourselves disgrace,
While self was ever the craving that in your spirits stirred,
Genius? A nonsense. Virtue? But a word.

O, leave in the old chronicles our forefathers to rest;
For they would gaze upon you with irony at best.
Rise once more, o Tepes ! Take and divide these men

As lunatics and rogues in two big tribes, and then
In mighty, twin infirmaries by force both tribes intern,
And with a single faggot prison and madhouse burn.

Satire IV

See the tall and lonely castle mirrored in the placid lake,
'Neath those waters does its shadow through the ages never wake,
Silently above the pine-tress rise its ancient rampart stark,
Throwing wide a flood of shadow o'er the brooding waters dark.
Through the high and arched windows silver curtains one can see,
Like the hoar frost coldly shining, hanging folds of drapery.
Slowly climbing up the heavens shows the moon behind the pines,
And the rocky crags and tree tops on the silver sky designs,
While the mighty oaks encircling like a watching giant band
Round, as though around some treasure, silent guard of honour stand.
Only the white swans that slowly through the rushes take their way,
Emperors of that lonely water, hold their proud and silent sway,
Now, as though to mount the heavens, spreading wide their mighty wings
Do they beat the water's surface, breaking it in silver rings,
While the sleeping rushes shiver giving forth a secret sight
And in the flower-sprinkled grass does a cricket sound its cry;
There's sweet sound and so much scent and so much summer in the air...

Beneath the hidden balcony a lonely knight is standing there,
The balcony hung o'er with leaves, in clusters round its pillars twined
Roses of Shiraz in bloom, and creeping plants of diverse kind;
While he intoxicated by the breeze that off the sleeping water strays
Amidst fair nature's magic spell on his guitar a nocturne plays.
"Beloved, show thyself again in thy long flowing silken gown
Which clinging close about thee seems with silver dust to be weighed down.
My whole life would I gaze on thee, that dost a crown of radiance wear

When thou dost lift thy small white hand to smooth aside thy golden hair.
Come sport with me... and with my luck... throw from thy casement in the skies.
A little faded meadow flower that on thy swelling bosom lies,
So that in falling it may strike on my guitar a trembling sound.
So bright the darkness it does seem that silver snow lies on the ground.
If to the perfumed fastness of your curtained boudoir I might win
Intoxicated with the scent of snowy flaxen sheets within,
Cupid, that small bantering page, would hide between his hands flame the flame.
Of thy bright gleaming bedside lamp, my beauteous, my graceful dame !"
A gentle sound of rustling silk ... a form that moves the leaves between
Among the scarlet roses and the climbing deep blue creepers seen.
Among the flowers the maiden laughs, and leans her hand the bars above-
Sweet as the image of a saint the faces are of those that love-
She throws him down a crimson rose, then on her lips a finger lays
As though to chide him, yet the while soft words of passion says.
Then drawing back she disappears... sound of steps that come in haste...
And through the door she slips at last, the knight has taken her round the waist
And arm in arm they stride away... a pretty match they make withal
So lovely she, and he so young, and both of them so slim and tall.
Out of the shadow of the cliff, towards the open shining lake,
With loose and lazy flapping sails, their boat its gentle course does take
And slowly through the silver night, amid the sound of lapping oars,

They glide across a magic lake that lies between enchanted shores.

The moon now, to her fullness come, athwart the sky her lantern swings
And o'er the water, shore to shore, a path of silver brilliance flings

That she upon the ripples lays, as though by lips of fairies kissed,
She the child of heaven's clear, dream of everlasting mist.
Gradually her beam grows brighter, clearer still and still more clear,
While the farther hills upstanding in her gleam quite close appear,
Wider too the forest growing that does clothe the water's side,
Spreading 'neath the disc of heaven, Queen of all that shining tide.
The while, tall limes with shadows wide, their blossoms trailing to the ground,
Above the shady waters lean and through their leaves soft breezes sound,
While on the maiden's golden head many scented petals light.
Now does she place her slender hands about the neck of that fair knight
And raising up her face to his, tenderly she whispers this:
"Deep in my soul how wildly sweet the word upon thy red lip is.
And oh, to what a heaven high within thy mind thou lift thy slave,
Still is the yearning in thy heart the single happiness I have.
And with its gentle fire thy voice can hurt and fill my soul with fears,
For ours does seem a tale of lave passed dawn to us from bygone years.
A wondrous unspoken dream thy eyes that do so sadly yearn,
Within their humid, thirsty depths I am consumed and ever burn.
O, give me back your gleaming eyes and turn them not away from me,
An ever standing miracle shall their eternal darkness be,

Fain would I gaze till I grow blind beholding them. But listen now
How countless tress and ripples soft hold converse with the stars, and how
The woods with dark delirious joy are full, and how the azure springs
Speak to each other of our love amid their happy babblings,
While Lucifer is trembling midst the summits of the highest trees,
The whole wide earth, the lake, the sky, all are our accomplices.
Well may we loose the rudder and let the lazy oars lie still
That on the water's gentle breast the waves should bear us where they will,
No matter where the waters drive, no matter what the kind wind's breath,
For everywhere our joy will lie... little matter life or death."

....
....

Fanny, naught but fancy's farce. When ever we are alone we two,
How oft you take me on the lake, what seas and forests guide me through !
Where did you see these unknown lands of which you speak to me today?
And where these joys? Since then I deem five hundred years have passed away
Today one may not loose one's soul enchanted by a maiden's gaze,
Though sick with longing you may be, you will not gain such maiden's ways,
As with your arms about her neck, with mouth to mouth and breast to breast,
Her eyes are asking: "Tell me true, 'tis really me you love the best?"
Alas, your hand is scarce held out but opens the door and pour in through
A swarm of wretched relatives, some uncles, then an aunt or two.

You hang your head, grin bashfully, and silent ask the skies above
If there be not in all the world a quiet spot in which to love.
Like mummies brought from Egypt they, stiffly upright in their chairs,
While you with twisting fingers writhe, numbering your moustache's hairs,
Or roll unwanted cigarettes, or sit with clenched and folded hands
And show how sensible you are, who even cooking understands.

O, I am weary of a life composed of desilusion's stuff,
Of misery and bitter prose... of such a life I've had enough;
To hallow with so many tears an instinct so banal and vain,
An instinct that the birds have got, and every spring comes back again.
You do not live, another soul inspires you, lives in your stead,
Laughs with your mouth, is happy. He, and he it was who whispered.
Your lives are like the ripples which into oblivion run away,
Eternity is evil all, and sin, a demigod, holds sway.
Do you not realize your love is not your own, you madman you?
Do you not know what nonsense cheap you hold for marvels and are true?
Do you not realize that love is only one of nature's needs?
Do you not know it nurtures lives that have in them but Satan's seeds?
Do you not see your laughter is the source of your own children's tears?
Cain's influence is on the earth and still no end to it appears.
O, theatre of puppet plays full of the babble of mankind...
Like parrots, they a thousand jokes and endless nonsense tales unwind.
Yet understand they not at all the things they tell. An actor climbs
Upon the stage and tells himself again, again ten thousand times,
What every age has always said, what every age will always say

Until the sun dips in the sea upon the eve of judgement day.
O, do you dream when midst the clouds the moon her nightly course does steer.
Dream deep in your imagined world that you your maiden can ender?
At midnight wander through the snow along a frosty wind-swept road
And gaze through lighted windows at the lighted rooms of her abode?
You'd see her stand complacently with many a worthless waiting beau
There gathered round, and each in turn a little winsome ogle throw,
Hear clank of spurs, see silken gowns from which faint rustling murmurs rise,
The young men turn mustachios, the ladies rolling sheeplike eyes.
While she with amorous glance accepts their propositions at her ease,
You, with your stupid sentiments, would you before her doorway freeze?
O passionate and stubborn fool, to love her in this childish way
When she is cold and whimsical, and sudden as an April day.
You clasp together longing hands, a madman's dream does you enthral,
For you would take her in your arms, to have her and to hold her all,
As though a Parian marble fair, or canvas that Correggio wrought,
Cold and coquettish as she is. Believe me, 'tis a foolish thought.
Aye, the maiden I had dreamt of, who would of loves enchantment know,
Who when I sat enwrap in thought would lean upon my shoulder so
That I would feel her presence near, and know I understood at last
To make of living but a tale, a life in happy legend past.
I seek no more. What should I seek? The same old song of my desire,

The hunger for eternal peace that sets my wretched soul afire.
The silver chords are broken now, my lyre no more of love does sing,
And yet the ancient song I hear sometimes at night beside the spring

Where, here and there, amidst the dark, a gleam of milk-white moonlight strays
From out a Carmen seculare as I did dream in former days...
But for this sad sigh and wailing, whistling, discordant sound,
Scattered cries and tangled noises in my weeping lyre are found.
Through my mind a breeze of winter sadly is a journey wending,
And around me chants forever tale of time inept unending.

What the outcome of existence? Where the message that I had?
All the lyre's chords are broken, and the minstrel man is mad.

Delilah (Satire V)

The Bible tells of Samson's wife that she deprived him of his power
By cutting off his hair while he did sleep, and that his foes that hour
Quick fell upon him, bound him hand and foot, and branded out his eyes,
Which shows what quality of soul is had beneath sweet woman's guise.
Young men, you, who filled with dreams' enchantment, a woman's graces would fain,
When glows the moon's bright golden shield o'er field and sylvan lane
And splashes on the earth green shadows that with mystery are fraught
Remember that a woman's skirts are long, her understanding short.
For you are drunken with the magic of a wondrous summer dream
That in you is lighted... But ask her longing, and I deem
That she will speak to you of frills and bows, and of the latest mode,
While secretly within your heart there beats the rhythm of an ode.
So, when she leans upon you fondlingly and fills you with her spells,
Beware 'tis demon lore. Think what the Bible of Dlilah tells.

She is winsome, it is understood, and childish are her wiles,
Sweet girlish dimples still adorn her cheeks whene'er she smiles,
And there are dimples at the corners of her mouth that murder hides,
And on each finger there are dimples too, and many more besides.
Not too small, and not too portly, not too slight, yet slim of waist,
Just an armful for a lover, just designed to be embraced;
All she says seems to become her, all she does befits her too,
All she wears sits well upon her, just as though it were her due.

When she speaks her voice is pleasing, even her silence does endear,
Though her words may say "Get from me," will her smile say "No, come here!"
And her stride is smooth as music, music rustles from her dress.
Languorous in every movement, always courting a caress.
Till, when rising on her tiptoes for her lips to reach your own,
She will kiss you with a secret warmth and mystery unknown,
A secret warmth that nowhere else than in a woman's soul can burn.
O, ravishing indeed the bliss that you imagine you will learn
When in her circling arms you watch the glow of love her cheeks engage!
She-so queenlike and so wayward; you - more fervent than her page.
You will fancy in your rapture when you gaze into her eyes
You have learned to value living right, and even death appraise.
And thus poisoned by a delicate, agreeable dejection,
You will see in her the reigning queen of your sad mind's affection
And fancying for you are shed the tears that on her lashes gleam,
Far more beautiful than Venus Anadyomene she will seem;
Until lost in lote's oblivion, where the hours take swiftest flight,
Every day she will grow dearer, more adored every night.

Illusion ! How don't you understand? The expression of her gentle face
Is nothing but a mask, a lie; her smile, her sadness, a grimace.
How don't you see to make believe, to cheat is all her heart's concern
And that you give your very soul to her, but get naught in return.
Vain indeed the seven-stringed lyre, true companion of your wooing,
Sings unheard with sombre cadence the complaint of your undoing.
O'er your eyes a veil of fable with deft fingers she has lain

As when the frosty flowers of winter spread their wonder o'er the pane,
While in your heart still summer blows; until you cry "Dear love allow
My flowing tears to bless with pious bitter reverence your brow !"
How should she guess it is a demon in your heart that does pursue
Her charm with such strange thirsty fire; a demon in your heart, not you;
And that this demon laughing, weeping tears unable to restrain

Would but capture her in order that he might himself explain.
Like a struggling armless sculptor in his torment does he seem,
Or a composer deaf becoming at the moment all supreme
When at last he hears the music of the planets on their courses
Born of cosmic gravity and flying centrifugal forces.
Little does she guess that demon is but for his model wooing;
Marble she with eyes of shadow and a voice like pigeons cooing.
Nor does he require that she upon a sacrificial altar die,
As was the sacred ritual custom once in ages long gone by
When a virgin for the model of a goddess had been chosen
And her graceful living loveliness in deathless marble frozen.

But to understand himself this demon would from death arise,
Ravished by the fire within him, thus himself to recognize;
Painting then his longing ardour and his passion's thirsty flow
In divine adonic verses, as did Horace long ago.
He would draw from vision's wonder many a leaping woodland stream,
Humid, shady forest dingle, stars that in the distance gleam,
Until that strange and secret moment of the birth of fairy rhymes
When in his dreams is recreated fairest dream of ancient times.
While with passion deep unbridled he will gaze on her adoring
And within her eyes so childish, sweet salvation there imploring.
In his arms would he embrace her while the endless ages rolled,

Melt beneath his burning kisses eyes that shine a radiance cold;
For indeed with so much loving melt at last would heart of stone,
When before her humbly kneeling he entreats in humble tone.
Happiness his soul consuming, he grows mad beneath love's thrill,
Midst the tempest of his passion, that grows ever wilder still.
Does she guess a single moment she could give the world entire
Should she let the waves engulf her and content his heart's aspire,
She could flood with starry wonder depths of nameless solitude?

With a smile of courtesan, but with timid eyes and prude,
She pretends to understand him. Women all soon flattered are
And will be so long as beauty blows upon this star.
A woman among flowers, a flower among a thousand women is she
And will please to endless time. But let her take a choice of three
Who standing round all tell her that they love her true, and she, so naive,
All of a sudden, you behold, becomes most strangely positive.
She may take for a screen your spirit and heart
Behind which she lures a young suitor, attractive and smart,
Who walks in like an actor, with light steps,
Floating in a wave of spicy fragrance and of chats,
Staring at her through his glasses, a pink in his buttonhole,
He is in clothing and in spirit a perfectly tailored work;
All the four kings of the cards may do for her game
And so their place in her heart's pantry is the same...
When does my lady gently flirt with eyes both innocent and coy,
Dividing up her favours 'twixt an aged rake and unfledged boy,
Her heart does not deceive her, nor subtle understanding cheat
To mix the knave of spades or diamonds with a knave out of the street
Before your wild demonic longing she will like a hermit speak,

But when appears the knave of spades the youthful blood mounts to her cheks
And soon her frosty shining eyes his sombre heart with fire accost,
And you will see her sitting there, one leg upon the other crossed,
The weak in wisdom are instead sometimes beautiful forsooth...

The dream that strong, outspoken fact or any manifested truth
Has power upon this world to change the trend of things in any wise,
This is the time-old stumbling-block that in the path of progress lies.

And so young man, when filled with dreams' enchantment you a woman's graces would fain,
When glows the moon's bright golden shield o'er field and sylvan lane
And splashes on the earth green shadows that with mystery are fraught,

Remember that a woman's skirt is long, her understanding short.
For you are drunken with the magic of a wondrous summer dream
That in you is lighted...
But ask her of her longing, and I deem
That she will speak to you of frills and bows, and of the latest mode,
While secretly within your heart there beats the rhythm of an ode ...
When you see a stone unfeeling, which for pity has no care,
Pause if there's a demon in you, 'tis Delilah, so take care!

'Tis eve on the hillside

'Tis eve on the hillside, the bagpipes are distantly wailing,
Flocks going homewards, and stars o'er the firmament sailing,
Sound of the bubbling spring sorrow's legend narrating,
And beneath a tall willow for me, dear one, you are waiting.

The wandering moon up the heavens her journey is wending,
Big-eyed you watch through the boughs her gold lantern ascending,
Now over the dome of the sky all the planets are gleaming,
And heavy your breast with its longing, your brow with its dreaming,

Corn-fields bright flooded with beams by the clouds steeply drifted,
Old cottage gables of thatch to the moonlight uplifted,
The tall wooden arm of the well in the wind softly grating,
And the shepherd-boy's pipe from the sheep-pen sad doina relating.

The peasants, their scythes on their backs, from their labour are coming.
The sound of the toaca its summons more loudly is drumming,
While the clang of the village church bell fills the evening entire,
And with longing for you like a faggot my soul is on fire.

O, soon will the village be silent and scarce a light burning,
O, soon eager steps to the hillside again 'Ill be turning,
And all the night long I will clasp you in love's hungry fashion,
And in secret we'll tell to each other the tale of our passion.

Till at last we will fall fast asleep neath the shade of that willow,
Your lips drawn aside in a smile and your breast for my pillow,
O, to live one such beautiful night all these wonders fulfilling
And barter the rest of existence, who would not be willing?

You never knew my soul

For me in all existence nowhere such wealth abides
As in the tender secret your gentle beauty hides;
For on what other wonder than that of your sweet charm
Would I a lifetime squander of meditation calm

On legends and on musing, and thus a language mould
That it with fleeting cadence your loveliness enfold
With chains of flowing images, and on it dreams bestow
That it ne'er till time's ending shall to the darkness go?
....
Today when all my being to your being is bound,
When hid in every sorrow for me a joy is found;
When you to me more lovely than marble do appear
And in your eye is kindled a ray of starlight clear
That while I gaze upon you I feel I must go blind
With so much shining wonder that floods upon my mind;

Today when is my longing so tender and so true
As is the very charm itself that does your form endue,
And stronger is the yearning that our two hearts have known
Than light that yearns for darkness, the chisel for the stone;
When my desire is boundless, so gentle and so high

As on the earth is nowhere, and nowhere in the sky;
When everything about you for me is magic spell,
A smile, a word, a gesture, no matter ill or well;
When you are the enigma of life for me the whole,
Your words now show me plainly you never knew my soul.

Of all the ships

Of all the ships the ocean rolls
How many find untimely graves
Piled high by you upon the shoals,
O waves and winds, o winds and waves?

How many a bird that leaves its bower
And o'er the sky in autumn droves
You beat and blindly overpower,
O waves and winds, o winds and waves?

Should easy luck or high endeavour
Be our aim it little saves,
For you pursue our footsteps ever,
O waves and winds, o winds and waves?

Still, it is past our comprehending
What design your song enslaves,
Rolling on until time's ending,
O waves and winds, o winds and waves?

Fair love, our mutual friend

Fair love, our mutual friend, took wing,
That is the reason why
My melancholy song must sing
To all the world goodbye.

Frail memory's cold finger tip
Will shut the past away,
That it no more shall cross my lips,
Nor through my spirit stray.

How many a murmuring of streams,
How many starlit flowers,
How many, many lover's dreams
I've buried with the hours.

To what unfathomed depth unknown
Had they their roots in me;
And, wetted by my tears, have grown,
Beloved one, for thee.

Through what sad torment did they rear,
Their blossoms to fulfil;
And, oh, how sorry am I, dear,
That I don't suffer still.

But you are now for ever gone,
Death called you very far;
And those gay eyes that glory shone
Now full of darkness are.

Your wistfully enchanted smile
Did somehow know, it seem,
To make of dream real life a while,
And out of life a dream.

And now I feel that you must dwell
Where the moon brightly lights
That country which the legends tell

Of thousand and one nights.

Love's mystery was too complete,
Too gentle and too strong;
A dream too wonderfully sweet
That it could last for long.

Maybe too much an angel you,
Too little just a girl,
That this strange ecstasy we knew
Its wings so soon should furl.

Too much dear one both you and I
In love's embrace were blind;
Too much forgot the lord on high
Too much forgot mankind.

Maybe indeed there is no room
In a world filled with distress,
Midst so much grief, and so much gloom,
For so much happiness.

Angel and Demon

Blackness of the cathedral dome, saddened by the yellow light
Of waxen candles shimmering, which burn before the altars' face;
While in the dark and spacious vault, unpenetrated realms of space
Defy the tapers' tired eyes that strain to probe unconquered night.

And empty is the twilight church, save where, upon the marble stair,
A child who like an angel kneels with deeply bowed and fervent head.
Upon the altar stands, amidst the rosy light the tapers shed,
With calm, pale face and gentle mean an image of the virgin fair.

Within a sconce upon the wall a guttering candle burns and drips
And gleaming drops of molten pitch hiss as they fall upon the ground.
While wreaths of dry and withered flowers emit a gentle rustling sound.
And the maiden's secret prayer rests silently upon her lips.

Sunk in the outer ring of dark, a marble cross his form concealing,
Wrapped in the shadow's heavy cloak, He like a demon silent stands,
His elbows resting on the cross and hanging down his tapered han
His eyes deep sunken in his head, his furrowed brow strange grief revealing.

Against the cross's chilly neck his burning cheek he thoughtfully lays;
About its snowy arms is looped his long and raven hair.
The sad light of the candle glow scarce reaches to the corner where

Upon his drawn and pallid face fall feebly its yellow rays.

She... an angel praying heaven -- He... a demon wrapped in woes;
She... the pure, the golden hearted -- He. . . not heeding heaven's loss.
He... in deathly shadow leaning on the cold arms of the cross --
While from the sad Madonna's feet his simple prayer to heaven goes.

Upon the wall by which she kneels, the high coal wall of marble fine
That shines as does the mountain snow, that as calm water turns the light,
Clearly as on a mirror falls the shadow of that maiden white,
Her bending shadow, like herself, kneeling in prayer before the shrine.

O what can ail thee, maiden sweet, with thy so gentle noble mien?
Pale is thy face as is the snow, and pale as wax thy tapered hands.
As river mist shot through with stars that on the hills at evening stands,
So shine thy innocent, soft eyes, beneath their veiling lashes seen.

Angel thou art, yet something lacks; an angel's tall, star-spattered wings.
But as I gaze I see take shape about your shoulders flying lines;
What are they, trembling in the air? Whence come these feathery designs?
An angel's pinion in the dusk towards the gate of heaven springs.

O, but the shadow is not hers; her guardian angel hovers there;
Against the whiteness of the wall I see his radiant figure tower.
Over the maiden's sinless life he watches with celestial power,

And as she bows her head to pray, he too is bowed in fervent prayer.

But if this be an angel's wing, then She too angel is; for though
The airy brightness of her wings is not revealed to eyes of man,
These walls alone, where age long prayer has been poured out in worship, can
Proclaim to us her angelhood and of her wings existence show.

I love, I love thee fain would cry the demon from the twilight shade,
But the winged shadow guarding her the utterance of his spirit sealed.
The passion died upon his lips; in worship not in love he kneeled
And heard across the hollow nave her timid murmur as she prayed.

....

She? A princess fair as day, a crown of stars upon her head!
All angel in a woman's guise, going her happy way through life.
He? A rebel of mankind, blowing to flame the sparks of strife
And sowing hate in hopeless breasts that to revolt by him are led.

Their ways of life are worlds apart, deep oceans lie between these twain,
Between them barricades of thought, the bitter bloodshed of a race.
And yet at times their journeys cross, they meet each other face to face,
Their eyes seek out each other's soul and mingle with a curious pain.

With gentle yet absorbing gaze, her large and starlike deep blue eyes
Rest thoughtfully on his that do the tempest and the lightning show.
While on his pallid face there mount emotions warm and tender glow.

They love... and yet what worlds apart, what universe between them lies.

A monarch pale has come from far, a time old crown he humbly brings;
The victor in a hundred wars, his conquests would he make her own.
He begs to lead her as his bride along the carpet to his throne
And place within her tiny hand the sceptre of the king of kings.

But no, with parted lips she turns and does not speak the fatal word;
Her heart is silent in her breast and from the king she draws her hands,
Her virgin soul is filled with love, while in her dreams there ever stands
The demon's image like a god, for every night his voice she heard.

She seems to see him leading men with words of fire, with winged ideas;
How brave, how powerful, how grand -- she thought in lovers' proud delight;
He leading on the rising age to conquer and to claim its right
Against the lifeless piled up weight of wisdom that experience rears.

She saw him standing on a rock, wrapt like a garment with his wrath
As with his banner's scarlet folds, his beetling forehead deeply scoured
As though a black tempestuous night when all the host of hell's aboard.
Out of his eyes the lightning gleamed, intoxicating words poured forth.
....
....

On a bed of boards the young man lies stretched in the agony of death,

Beside his couch a dim lamp burns, its poor thin wick and meagre flame
Struggle against the cold damp air. No mall has ever heard his name,
None comes to ease his bitter lot, or wet his lips that choke for breath.

O past are the days when in the world the thunder of his voice would roll
Against the written codes of law, against the laws that bound and maimed,
And slew men in the name of God... today the world's revenge is aimed
Upon the dying heretic, and stifles out his stricken soul.

To die bereft of every hope, what man is there on earth who knows
The awful meaning of these words? To feel enslaved and weak and small,
To fight and hope and see your plans shrivelled to nothing after all,
To know that in the world is throned an evil force none may oppose.

Your years were spent in strife with wrong, and you a useless fight have fought,
And now you die and see your life was wrecked in work without avail,
Such death is Hell. More bitter tears than these ne'er coursed the visage pale
Of dying man. How cruel to know that you and all the world are naught.

Such black thoughts rising in his soul delay the death for which he yearns.
With what great gifts has he been born. What passionate love of right and truth,
What sympathy for human kind, and all the lofty flame of youth.
Behold his recompense at last, this agony with which he burns.

But into that narrow tawdry room, breaking the mist that veiled his eye,
A silver shadow softly creeps; behold, an angel shape comes near,
Sits lightly on the wretched bed, kisses away each blinding tear
From those dimmed eyes; and now the mist is torn away in ecstasy.

Aye, it is She. And with what joy, joy fathomless, before unknown,
He gazes in his angel's face and reads love's tender pity there.
With long glance he is repaid all his life's anguish and despair.
He whispers with his dying breath "My love I know thee for my own.

I who have laboured all my life poor and helpless souls to move,
Warring against the open skies with all my burning discontent;
A demon, yet not cursed by God, for in my dying hour he sent
His angel here to give me peace, and of his peace the name is love.

So long, dear one, since you departed

So long, dear one, since you departed,
Since last we spoke it is so long,
I feel as though I have forgotten
How our love was blind and strong.

Today again you sit before me;
Pallidly, yet ever so sweet ...
Let me now, as I was wonted,
Kneel down humbly at your feet.

Let me weep for you my pity,
Kiss your fingers one by one.
O little hands, my own beloved,
Through all these weeks what have you done?

Return

Forest, trusted friend and true,
Forest dear, how do you do?
Since the day I saw you last
Many, many years have passed
And though you still steadfast stand
I have travelled many a land."

"Yea, and I, what have I done?
Watched the years their seasons run;
Heard the squalls that through me groan
Ere my singing birds have flown;
Heard the creaking of my boughs
Neath the mounted winter snows.

Yea indeed, what have I done?
Done as I have always done;
Felt my summer leaves re-growing,
Heard the village girls who going
By the path that meets the spring
Melancholy doina sing".

"Forest, though the tempests blow,
The years come and the years go.
And the seasons wax and wane,
You are ever young again".

'"What of seasons, when for ages
All the sky my lake engages;
What of years ill or good,
When the sap mounts in the wood!
What of years good or ill,
When the Danube rolls on still.
Only mall is always changing,
O'er the world forever ranging,
We each do our place retain,
As we were, so we remain;
Oceans, rivers, mountains high
And the stars that light the sky,
Saturn with its whirling rings,

And the forest with its springs.

One wish alone have I

One wish alone have I:
In some calm land
Beside the sea to die;
Upon its strand
That I forever sleep,
The forest near,
A heaven near,
Stretched o'er the peaceful deep.
No candles shine,
Nor tomb I need, instead
Let them for me a bed
Of twigs entwine.

That no one weeps my end,
Nor for me grieves,
But let the autumn lend
Tongues to the leaves,
When brooklet ripples fall
With murmuring sound,
And moon is found
Among the pine-trees tall,
While softly rings
The wind its trembling chime
And over me the lime
Its blossom flings.
As I will then no more
A wanderer be,
Let them with fondness store
My memory.
And Lucifer the while,
Above the pine.
Good comrade mine,
Will on me gently smile;
In mournful mood,
The sea sing sad refrain...
And I be earth again
In solitude.

Thank you!

We hope you enjoyed our product.

As we constantly want to improve our work, your feedback is very important to us.

Please let us know any suggestions, how you like our book, questions at:

contact.keelanthome@gmail.com

www.ingramcontent.com/pod-product-compliance
Lightning Source LLC
Chambersburg PA
CBHW050302120526
44590CB00016B/2461

© Copyright 2022 - All rights reserved.

You may not reproduce, duplicate or send the contents of this book without direct written permission from the author. You cannot hereby despite any circumstance blame the publisher or hold him or her to legal responsibility for any reparation, compensations, or monetary forfeiture owing to the information included herein, either in a direct or an indirect way.

Legal Notice: This book has copyright protection. You can use the book for personal purpose. You should not sell, use, alter, distribute, quote, take excerpts or paraphrase in part or whole the material contained in this book without obtaining the permission of the author first.

Disclaimer Notice: You must take note that the information in this document is for casual reading and entertainment purposes only. We have made every attempt to provide accurate, up to date and reliable information. We do not express or imply guarantees of any kind. The persons who read admit that the writer is not occupied in giving legal, financial, medical or other advice. We put this book content by sourcing various places.

Please consult a licensed professional before you try any techniques shown in this book. By going through this document, the book lover comes to an agreement that under no situation is the author accountable for any forfeiture, direct or indirect, which they may incur because of the use of material contained in this document, including, but not limited to, —errors, omissions, or inaccuracies.

WorldWide Spark Publish